Global Cities
CAPE TOWN

Rob Bowden
photographs by Roy Maconachie

CHELSEA HOUSE
PUBLISHERS
An imprint of Infobase Publishing

Cape Town

Chelsea House
An imprint of Infobase Publishing
132 West 31st Street
New York NY 10001

Library of Congress Cataloging-in-Publication Data
Bowden, Rob.
  Cape Town / Rob Bowden ; photographs by Roy Maconachie.
     p. cm. -- (Global cities)
  Includes bibliographical references and index.
  ISBN 0-7910-8856-1 (acid-free paper)
  1. Cape Town (South Africa)--Juvenile literature. I. Title. II. Series.
  DT2405.C364B68 2006
  968.73'55--dc22

                              2006045487

Chelsea House books are available at special discounts when purchased in bulk quantities for businesses, associations, institutions, or sales promotions. Please call our Special Sales Department in New York at (212) 967-8800 or (800) 322-8755.

You can find Chelsea House on the World Wide Web at http://www.chelseahouse.com.

Printed in China.

10 9 8 7 6 5 4 3 2 1

This book is printed on acid-free paper.

Design: Robert Walster, Big Blu Design
Maps and graphics: Matt Darlinson

All photographs are by Roy Maconachie (EASI-Images) except the following: 14 left, 31 inset, 34 left, 36 bottom, 40 top, 48 bottom, 50 top, by Tony Binns (EASI-Images); and 13 left, 41, 46 top, and 48 left, by Corbis.

First published by Evans Brothers Limited
2A Portman Mansions, Chiltern Street, London W1U 6NR, United Kingdom

This edition published under licence from Evans Brothers Limited. All rights reserved.

All links and web addresses were checked and verified to be correct at the time of publication. Because of the dynamic nature of the web, some addresses and links may have changed since publication and may no longer be valid.

Contents

Living in an urban world

As of 2007 the world's population will, for the first time in history, be more urban than rural. An estimated 3.3 billion people will find themselves living in towns and cities such as Cape Town, and for many the experience of urban living will be relatively new. For example, in China, the world's most populous country, the number of people living in urban areas increased from 196 million in 1980 to more than 536 million in 2005.

The urban challenge...

This staggering rate of urbanization (the process by which a country's population becomes concentrated into towns and cities) is being repeated across much of the world and presents the world with a complex set of challenges for the 21st century. Many of these challenges are local, such as the provision of clean water for expanding urban populations, but others are global in scale. In 2003 an outbreak of the highly contagious disease SARS demonstrated this as it spread rapidly among the populations of well-connected cities around the globe. The pollution generated by urban areas is also a global concern, particularly because urban residents tend to generate more than their rural counterparts.

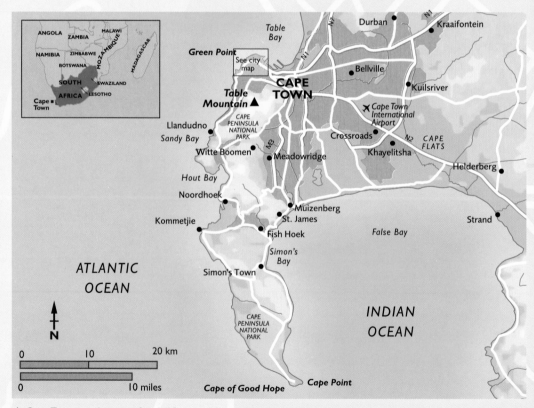

▲ Cape Town in relation to South Africa and its neighboring countries.

... and opportunity!

Urban centers, and particularly major cities like Cape Town, also provide great opportunities for improving life at both a local and global scale. Cities concentrate people and allow for efficient forms of mass transportation such as subway or light rail networks. Services too, such as waste collection, recycling, education, and health care can all function more efficiently in a city. Cities are centers of learning, and they are often the birthplace of new ideas, ranging from innovations in science and technology to new ways of day-to-day living. Cities also provide a platform for the celebration of arts and culture, and as their populations become more multicultural such celebrations are increasingly global in their reach.

▼ Cape Town grew because of ocean connections with the wider world. Today its maritime industries remain, but it has also become a center for business, commerce, and tourism.

A global city

Although all urban centers share certain things in common, there are a number of cities in which the challenges and opportunities facing an urban world are particularly condensed. These can be thought of as global cities, cities that in themselves provide a window on the wider world and reflect the challenges of urbanization, of globalization, of citizenship, and of sustainable development that face us all. Cape Town is one such city. It is one of the most important cities in Africa and the focal point of a new South Africa emerging from almost half a century of apartheid. Its people live with the burden of a turbulent past but at the same time demonstrate great enthusiasm for the future of their city and their country. This book introduces the city and its people, investigates just what makes Cape Town a truly global city, and explores how its residents are facing the future.

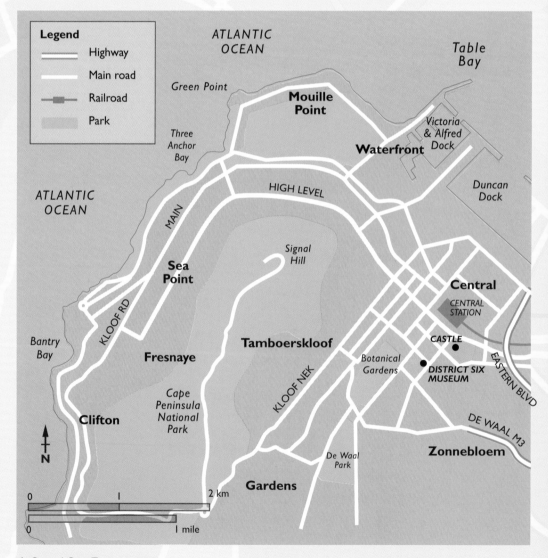

▲ Central Cape Town.

An African leader

Cape Town is situated close to the southern tip of the African continent, and this position has long made it an important point of contact between Africa and the outside world. It was in Cape Town, for example, that some of the first European settlers arrived in 1652, and the city soon established itself as a key port for the export of Africa's riches.

Cape Town maintains a prominent position in Africa today. Although it is not among the continent's most populous cities, Cape Town is one of the most important in political and economic terms. It is the legislative capital of South Africa (Africa's most powerful nation) and the seat of a government that many consider to be setting the standards for Africa in the 21st century. Cape Town also remains a major port and in recent decades has developed

▲ Cape Town faces a housing shortage. Many poor residents are crammed into informal settlements such as this one at New Rest on the Cape Flats.

into a global business and commercial center. Cape Town has also become a major tourist location and frequently ranks as one of the world's most desirable tourist destinations.

A local challenge

But Cape Town is not without its challenges. It remains a city divided by the legacy of apartheid, where the wealthy districts of Camps Bay and the Waterfront seem worlds apart from the impoverished living conditions of the Cape Flats settlements like Khayelitsha. These divides and the struggle for greater integration are at the core of many other challenges facing the city. Among these are the threat posed by HIV/AIDS, the degradation of the local environment, and serious concerns about law and order.

◄ An old Cape Dutch house in the Observatory neighborhood of the wealthy southern suburbs.

The history of Cape Town

Prehistoric evidence suggests the earliest human settlement in the Cape region dates back more than 100,000 years. Most historic accounts, however, begin at the point of contact with Europe in the late 15th century. At this time the Khoisan were the dominant ethnic group of the region and lived in small numbers (a few hundred are recorded by early European travelers) with a livelihood based upon hunting and gathering, and herding. The Portuguese trader Bartolomeu Dias was the first European to make contact with southern Africa, rounding the Cape of Good Hope in 1488. Dias was not interested in the Cape itself but in the lucrative trade of Asia to the east, to which the Cape provided a gateway. Other European traders soon followed Dias around the Cape, often making for harbor in Table Bay to resupply their ships with fresh water, food, and provisions.

▼ Once a vegetable garden for the first European settlers, the Botanical Gardens in the heart of Cape Town are now the city's best-known green space.

The first settlers

In 1652 Dutch traders began to settle in the Cape region. Jan van Riebeeck of the Dutch East India Company established a supply station for ships making the voyage between Holland and the East Indies. He built a fort and established a vegetable garden (the site of today's Botanical Gardens) to meet these needs. By 1657 employees of the Dutch East India Company had begun to settle as farmers in the surrounding area, and by 1658 the company was importing slaves (mainly Asians from the East Indies) to meet the increasing demand for labor.

▼ The docks of the Alfred Basin were developed in the 1860s to boost trade in Cape Town. Today they are only used by smaller vessels and pleasure craft.

The British and the Boers

Cape Town's importance in controlling the sea route to the east made it a prize for competing European powers. The Dutch East India Company maintained control, however, until a British force took the city in 1795. The Dutch regained control for a brief period in 1803–06, but Cape Town then passed back into British hands and became part of the British Empire from 1814. The British had abolished the slave trade in 1807, and in 1834 Cape Town's slaves were freed and given the right to own land in the Cape Colony. The resident Dutch population (by then known as Boers or Afrikaners after the language they had developed) rejected British control and began a mass migration inland known as the Great Trek.

Cape Town flourished under the British, who built a railroad to the interior and improved port facilities during the 1860s. The discovery of diamond (1870)

and gold (1886) deposits inland further boosted Cape Town as a major port, but competition over this mineral wealth led to a war between the British and the Boers. The Boers had established independent republics (Transvaal and Orange Free State) following their trek inland from the Cape. The Boer War (1899–1902) was won by the British and led to the eventual unification of South Africa in 1910. Cape Town was chosen as the new legislative capital—a position it still holds.

▶ This 1929 photograph shows the busy docks of the Victoria and Alfred Basins. The large building is a grain silo.

The apartheid era

Defeated in the Boer War, the Afrikaner population (mainly descendants of the original Dutch settlers and Boer Trekkers) found themselves competing for jobs with the black and colored (mixed race) populations they had previously controlled. Many Afrikaners found this situation unsatisfactory and began an Afrikaner nationalist movement, which eventually led to the creation of the National Party. The National Party came to power in 1948 and in 1950 formalized a system of racial segregation in South Africa that they called apartheid, meaning "to keep apart."

Apartheid created a white-controlled South Africa unfairly segregated by race (white, colored, and black). A series of Land Acts in 1950, 1954, and 1955 determined where people could live and work according to the color of their skin, and the Pass Laws of 1952 restricted the movement of the black and colored populations beyond their own areas. Everything became segregated—from public benches and restrooms to entire education systems.

Cape Town underwent considerable transformations as a result of apartheid. District Six, a thriving and cosmopolitan

▲ During the apartheid era Thulani Mabaso was imprisoned on Robben Island for 18 years. Today he guides tourists around the former prison.

part of the city, was severely affected when it was declared a white area in 1966. The 60,000 nonwhite residents, some of whose families had been there for several generations, were relocated to black and colored townships and their homes and business demolished. This process was repeated in other parts of the city and led to the formation of poorly serviced and overcrowded slum areas, such as Crossroads near the city's airport.

▼ This historical image shows prisoners being transported to the infamous apartheid-era jail on Robben Island.

District Six

Joe Schaffers works as a guide at the District Six Museum, in the center of Cape Town. He is one of the thousands of residents who were forcibly evicted from the district during the apartheid era. He was relocated to the Cape Flats, where he worked as a health inspector and saw the terrible conditions that many former residents of District Six had to put up with. Joe recalls how the clearance of District Six destroyed not only buildings, but also one of Cape Town's oldest and closest communities. "People were spread across the vast Cape Flats and the sense of community was lost," he says, "but since the end of apartheid around 4,000 people, mostly elderly now, have returned to live here in District Six." Joe explains that there is still a sense of pride and belonging when it comes to District Six, and the museum tries to capture some of this as a reminder not only of Cape Town's turbulent past, but also how it could be.

▼ Joe Schaffers stands next to some of the original street signs from District Six.

▲ Poverty and poor living conditions are a major concern in Cape Town. Despite the end of apartheid, the black population remains the most disadvantaged.

Resisting apartheid

The apartheid era met with widespread opposition, ranging from international sanctions against South Africa to locally led protests. As the seat of the government, Cape Town was frequently the target of this opposition, but it was an island in Table Bay, Robben Island, that really came to symbolize this era. It was there that anti-apartheid leaders, including Nelson Mandela, were imprisoned.

Cape Town came to the fore of the anti-apartheid movement in the 1980s, when the authorities tried to move people from Crossroads to another settlement just built at Khayelitsha. Resistance from the Crossroads residents, many of whom had been relocated before, escalated into a period of violence known as the Crossroads Clearances. At least 60 people died in clashes with the authorities; houses were burned to the ground; and around 60,000 people were forced to move.

A new era dawns

Not long after the Crossroads Clearances the apartheid era began to dissolve. The Pass Laws were revoked in 1986 and numerous anti-apartheid leaders were released from prison, including Nelson Mandela in 1990. By 1993 a new constitution had been written to affirm equal rights to all South Africans. This paved the way for the country's first free elections in 1994, when Nelson Mandela was elected president. This marked an end to the policies of apartheid, but the social divides created by more than 40 years of segregation are still evident today. In Cape Town these differences remain stark, with Cape Flats settlements like Khayelitsha being worlds apart from the white suburbs of Hout Bay.

Cape Town has, however, achieved a great deal since the end of apartheid. New businesses have been attracted to the city; rundown districts have been redeveloped; and there has been new investment in severely poor neighborhoods. Crime has been reduced too, a factor that has contributed to the city's growth as a tourist attraction.

◀ New homes in Cape Flats are a sign of the positive changes to have occurred in Cape Town since 1994.

▲ Once the preserve of the white community, desirable seaside houses can now be bought by anyone who can afford them.

Writing tomorrow's history

One of the most significant changes is to how the city is governed and managed. New systems have been put in place to make the city more accountable to its residents, such as the Junior City Council, which provides a platform for young people's concerns to be heard. Another significant change has been the amalgamation in 2000 of previously separate city authorities. It is hoped that a single municipal council, referred to locally as the "Unicity," will allow Cape Town to better deal with the challenges of today. Among the most serious of these are how to deal with population growth, provide services, promote equality, and cope with HIV/AIDS.

▲ Children at Observatory Junior School learn about HIV/AIDS.

The people of Cape Town

By the time of the Boer War (1899–1902) Cape Town had a population of around 100,000 people, but in the century that followed this rose dramatically.

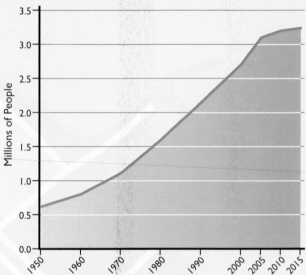

▲ Cape Town population growth, 1950–2015.

In the early to mid-1900s, rural migrants flocked to Cape Town to fill jobs being created there by the growth of industry and commerce. The majority of these migrants found work and settled in and around the city in the Cape Flats, substantially boosting its population. Cape Town is the economic hub of western South Africa, so it continues to attract migrants today. In addition, the natural increase of the resident population has added considerably to the number of people in the city. Relatively high birth rates have been exaggerated by the profile of migrants arriving in Cape Town: The majority are young and have yet to begin their families. By 1980 Cape Town had surpassed Johannesburg to become South Africa's largest city and remained so until 2000, by which time its population had reached 2.7 million. In 2005 Cape Town had a population of 3.1 million, slightly lower than Johannesburg, with 3.3 million.

▼ Members of an extended family enjoy their new home, built with funding from a national Reconstruction and Development Programme (RDP) to improve the lives of millions.

Urbanization

The rapid growth of Cape Town's population has placed extreme pressure on available housing and associated needs (water supplies, schools, hospitals, and so on). Hundreds of thousands of migrants have ended up living in poor-quality informal settlements, known locally as "pondokkies" (from *pondok,* the Afrikaans word for "hovel" or "hut"). The pondokkies are built of whatever scraps of material were available—wood, corrugated metal sheets, or sacking, for instance. They have no piped water, sewerage, or electricity and are prone to winter floods and summer fires. Several of Cape Town's townships have grown from former pondokkies. Many now have improved buildings, electricity, and water supplies, but others still lack such services and most remain overcrowded.

By 2003 an estimated 325,000 people, or around 10 percent of the city's population, were living in 71 informal settlements comprising 84,000 dwellings. In response Cape Town has identified a

▲ Cape Town's informal settlements make use of locally available materials such as scraps of corrugated metal sheets and abandoned wood.

need for at least 245,000 new houses, and in 2002 city authorities began work on a new City Housing Plan to meet this demand. An informal settlements upgrade program has also begun, the first phase of which is the introduction of emergency water, sanitation, and waste-disposal services. By 2004 more than 90 percent of residents in accessible settlements had been given these basic services, making the settlements more sustainable. The following phases will introduce permanent services to reduce the proportion of people living in informal settlements to 5 percent of the population by 2020.

◀ City authorities are coordinating the construction of new homes and the upgrading of existing dwellings.

Meeting the demand

Meeting the water, sanitation, and waste-collection needs of its population is especially important for Cape Town; failure to do so can result in considerable health problems. Many serious illnesses such as cholera, typhoid, and other diarrheal diseases are directly related to these factors and they have a particular impact on young children. In Khayelitsha and Nyanga, districts that lack many services, infant mortality rates are double those of much of the rest of the city. Providing the necessary infrastructure such as pipes, standpipes, public restrooms, and sewers is only part of the solution, however. Education is also important to increase awareness and inform people of how they can improve their living environments. In 2003 the city launched an environmental education and training strategy to educate communities about water and waste management.

▲ A Dumpster in Philippi collects communal trash, but there are too few Dumpsters available and the area around them is often littered with surplus refuse.

Water crisis

Water provision is an important challenge for Cape Town. The city is located in a dry area and most of its drinkable water comes from outside the city. Population growth, combined with increased demand from industry and commerce, has resulted in a serious water crisis in recent years. In 2000–01 water had to be restricted because of fears that the city's supplies might run out. This did not happen, and by 2002 the five major reservoirs supplying Cape Town had returned to full capacity. But in 2003 and 2004, below average rainfall over the winter (May–October) left the reservoirs less than half full by the end of October. Water restrictions were reintroduced and an appeal was made for citizens to help the authorities reach a 20 percent reduction in water use. A similar appeal in 2001 had been very successful.

◀ This display alerts people to Cape Town's water crisis. It uses one-liter water bottles to show that a shower can use almost 20 liters (about 5 gallons) of water a minute.

Citizenship

The strategy of local government working in partnership with local residents, as in the water crisis, has proved to be very effective. It has been used to develop plans for housing, environmental improvement, and pollution control. Where citizens have been involved there has been a greater sense of ownership and of pride in their city. The authorities have also become more open and enabled citizens to participate in ways that were not possible during the apartheid, for example, through contact centers and mayoral listening programs. The greater involvement of residents is also helping to bridge some of the gaps that exist between different racial groups.

▶ A man collects waste from a landfill site to sell for recycling—an informal activity that contributes to the management of the city.

▼ Women collect water from a public standpipe in Philippi.

Living in the city

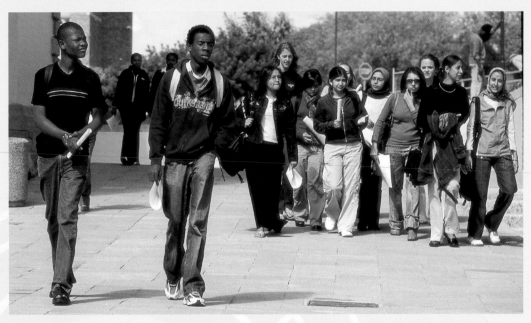

▲ Students of different racial makeup between classes at the University of Cape Town (UCT) campus.

Cape Town's history of contact with the outside world through conquest and trade has given it an especially diverse population. Black Africans (mainly Khoisan) were the original inhabitants of the Cape region, but today they are vastly outnumbered by South Africans of mixed race. In South Africa (but not elsewhere) mixed-race people are known as "colored."

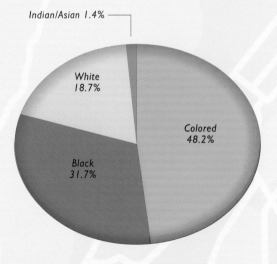

Indian/Asian 1.4%

White 18.7%

Colored 48.2%

Black 31.7%

▲ Ethnic composition of Cape Town (2001 census).

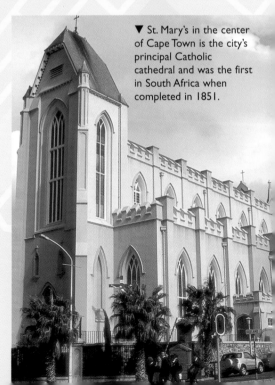

▼ St. Mary's in the center of Cape Town is the city's principal Catholic cathedral and was the first in South Africa when completed in 1851.

The colored population are descended from slaves imported from Asia (mainly Indonesia, Malaysia, and India) who intermarried with local Khoisan people. Also known as Cape coloreds or Cape Malays, the colored population compose almost half of the city population according to the 2001 census. Black Capetonians account for just under a third of the

▼ A Muslim woman and her grandson relax on their veranda in Bo-Kaap, a region with a large Muslim population.

population and whites for just under a fifth. There is a much smaller population of Indians, who make up about 1.5 percent of the populace. During apartheid these racial groups lived very separate lives. The physical barriers have long gone, but the economic, social, and cultural divides between the different groups are still evident today in issues such as housing, education, health, and employment.

Cape Town's religious composition reflects its diverse population, and there are at least 24 religious denominations. The majority of these are Christian, and Christianity accounts for around 76 percent of the total population. Islam is the next significant religion, practiced by just under 10 percent of the population. The Islamic community is particularly, but not exclusively, focused around the city's Bo-Kaap district. There are small numbers of Jews (0.5 percent) and Hindus (0.2 percent), and almost 11 percent of the population claim no religious affiliation.

▼ The mosque in Bo-Kaap. The brightly painted houses in the background are a distinctive feature of Bo-Kaap.

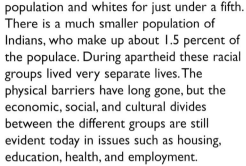

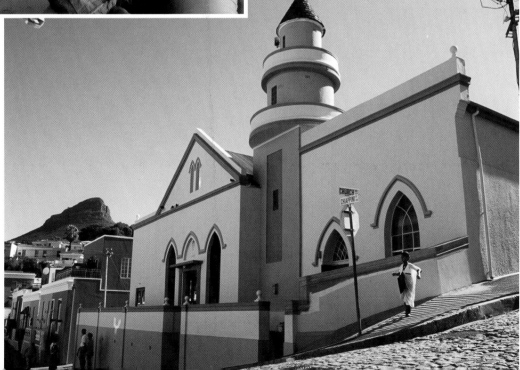

"Two cities in one"

Cape Town is frequently described as two cities in one. This refers to the differences that are visible between areas such as the upmarket Camps Bay and the slums of the Cape Flats. In reality there are many "cities" in between these extremes.

The differences in living standards by race are becoming less distinct as time passes, but inequalities remain stark. Average monthly incomes are one way to consider these inequalities. At the last census in 2001, 90 percent of black employees were in the lower income range of less than $400 per month. This compared with 74 percent of coloreds, 45 percent of Asians, and 26 percent of whites. At the other end of the earning scale only 1 percent of black employees earned in excess of $1,600 per month, compared with 1.8 percent of coloreds, 10.1 percent of Asians, and 20.3 percent of whites.

The disparities in wealth are mirrored by the quality of housing. In areas such as Clifton (to the south of the city center), grand mansions with swimming pools and sea views are in strong contrast to the overcrowded slums of Langa, Joe Slovo, and Khayelitsha. The provision and quality of health and education services also varies considerably. Among the white population for instance, 76 percent of those over 20 years of age have been educated to secondary level or above. The figure for the black population is just 26 percent, with 24 percent not having completed even their primary education.

CASE STUDY

CAFDA

Neil Scott is the director of the Cape Flats Development Association (CAFDA), one of the main organizations working to improve the lives of people living there. CAFDA's work is subsidized by the government, but to meet its 6 million rand ($960,000) annual budget, it must find 3.5 million ($560,000) from other sources. Neil explains, "We have 150 volunteers working for CAFDA and our projects cover communities with some 300,000 people." Among the projects CAFDA runs are job-creation projects (such as a bakery that trains bread makers and supplies pastries to a coffee shop), social work and community outreach programs, and a youth development center to try and keep young people off the streets. CAFDA has also built around 300 homes that are now owned by local residents, in an effort to ease the housing shortage. HIV/AIDS is always an issue in Cape Town, and CAFDA also runs awareness programs in the communities it works with.

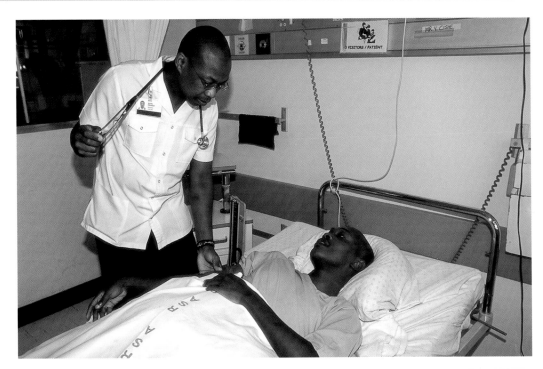

▲ A doctor monitors a patient at Cape Town's Groote Schuur Hospital, famous for doing the world's first-ever heart transplant. Despite such excellence many people in Cape Town lack access to even basic health care.

Equality for all

The Cape Town authorities are striving to reduce inequalities in the city by providing infrastructure and services to those areas and communities most in need. Health clinics in some wealthy areas have seen services reduced from daily to twice a week, for example. This allows valuable health resources to be focused on the more densely populated and needy areas such as Khayelitsha. In addition, new clinics are being built across the city as part of an equity policy to make sure no community is more than 1.5 miles (closer in areas of very high population density) from a primary health care clinic.

▶ A woman on a job creation project run by CAFDA learns new sewing skills.

A new beginning

In November 2000 a fire in Joe Slovo, an informal settlement on the outskirts of Cape Town, quickly spread out of control. The makeshift shacks of Joe Slovo were so densely packed that firefighters found it impossible to reach the blaze, and 980 homes were destroyed in just two hours. The fire also cut power to Cape Town, because Joe Slovo had been built on vacant land under the power cables. Industries and businesses were forced to close at enormous cost to the city economy. Joe Slovo was declared a disaster zone, but from the ashes a new beginning has arisen.

New land, away from the power lines, was allocated to those who lost their homes in Joe Slovo. The land was organized in blocks of around 100 shacks in a grid pattern with tracks left undeveloped between each block. The tracks form firebreaks to reduce destruction from any future fire and also allow fire, police, medical, and sanitation vehicles to enter the settlement, providing improved services to the community. Regular monthly meetings with city officials have allowed residents to be directly involved in decisions such as the location of new toilet facilities. Other improvements include electrification to reduce the need for open fires or kerosene lamps (both fire hazards) and standpipes to improve sanitation and save time in collecting water.

▲ City planners are looking for ways to improve life in Cape Town's informal settlements and townships.

▼ The installation of electricity supplies to Cape Town's slum settlements is one way of reducing the risk of fire by replacing kerosene as an energy source.

A new way of working

Private companies have also helped to develop Joe Slovo, recognizing their role as corporate citizens. A company called Santam and the newspaper *Cape Argus* helped fund a fire education and prevention project called Ukuvuka Operation Firestop to give each home information about fire prevention and action. Every shack now has a red bucket and whistle so that local people can raise the alarm and quickly mobilize to limit the spread of future fires. In 2001 another serious fire broke out in Joe Slovo, but rapid community action and improved access for firefighters limited the damage to just 30 shacks.

The electricity provider Eskom is another partner in Joe Slovo, running a greening program to turn the land under the power lines into vegetable gardens and playing fields. This benefits the residents of Joe Slovo and at the same time reduces the risks of future power interruptions for Eskom. Joe Slovo has become a model for other informal settlements and demonstrated a new way of working in

▲ City authorities are improving access to toilets in the townships (here in Philippi), but each toilet must still be shared by four families.

Cape Town. As one of the city officials summed it up, "The more we get involved, the more we talk to each other, the more we solve the problem."

▼ One of Cape Town's urban development policies is to create more public spaces for communities such as here in the Philippi township. This policy is known as the "Dignified Places" program.

Feeding the city

Cape Town's early role as a settlement was principally as a garden to supply food for passing ships. Cape Town now has some 3.1 million people to feed, and it is clear that this is impossible from the land within the city boundaries alone. Urban agriculture still plays a role in meeting food needs, however. Most urban agriculture is small-scale vegetable growing, but people also raise livestock (cows, chickens, pigs, goats, and sheep) in some of the Cape Flats settlements. In 2003 the city government launched an urban agriculture strategy. It works with urban farmers to make farming one of the ways to fight poverty and improve living standards. A third of the city population live below or just above the minimum household subsistence level (a level of income that allows them to meet basic needs).

Encouraging urban farming could dramatically improve the well-being of such people, and the benefits go far beyond providing food. Urban agriculture also frees up income, which can be spent on health care or education. If farmers grow surplus food it may even generate additional income. The Cape Town strategy will identify urban land for farming, provide tools to farmers, and carry out research and education to improve farming practices. It will also work with local initiatives like Abalimi Bezekhaya ("planters of the home"), a community-based organization that has been supporting urban farmers in the Cape Flats through resource centers and community gardens since 1982. The resource centers provide seeds, tools, manure, pest controls, and education and advice to more than 5,000 urban farmers a year and have recently established market days for farmers to sell their surplus produce.

▲ Local stalls throughout Cape Town sell seasonal fruit and vegetables produced in the Cape region.

▶ Urban agriculture can make a valuable contribution to the diet and income of poorer households.

The climate

Cape Town's climate is dominated by the oceans and mountains surrounding it. Cape Town does not experience real extremes of temperature or rainfall and can be described as a comfortable climate throughout the year. It is in the Southern Hemisphere, so winter is June to August, when rainfall peaks and temperatures reach their lowest. The summer is December to March, and although some days can be very hot (more than 30°C; 86°F) these are unusual. Wind is one of the main factors in Cape Town's climate, and strong winds of more than 75 miles per hour are not uncommon during the spring (September to November). The most famous wind is the Cape Doctor, a southeasterly wind that

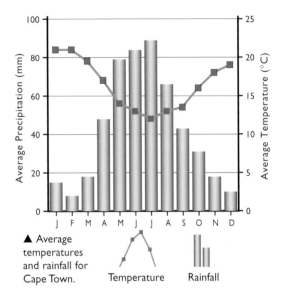

▲ Average temperatures and rainfall for Cape Town.

Temperature   Rainfall

is responsible for the formation of the famous "table cloth" cloud that drapes itself over Table Mountain and the city.

▼ The beaches of the Cape Peninsula provide an appealing way to cool off during the hot summer months.

The Cape Town economy

Cape Town accounts for 6.5 percent of South Africa's population, but its economic contribution is disproportionately higher at about 11 percent of national income. Cape Town has transportation, skills, and natural resource advantages that allow it to consistently outperform South Africa as a whole. Between 1991 and 2000 the Cape Town economy grew at an average annual rate of 2.6 percent, compared with an average expansion rate of 1.8 percent per year for the South African economy as a whole. Cape Town's future prospects look good too, with the local economy predicted to grow by more than 4 percent a year through 2010.

▲ Banks and offices dominate the central business district of Cape Town.

▲ Women lining up outside the employment office.

Not fast enough

Despite impressive growth figures, Cape Town's economy is not growing fast enough to create enough jobs for the new migrants. Experts say it will need to grow at around 7 percent a year if it is to generate enough jobs to absorb new entrants, let alone reduce unemployment in the city. Unemployment is currently around one fifth of the workforce, though this varies from 3 percent among the white population to 35 percent among the black population. One of the problems facing Cape Town is that many of the industries driving economic growth are also adopting labor-saving production methods, which means that new job creation is low.

Economic structure

In terms of their economic contribution, the main sectors in Cape Town are manufacturing (especially of electronics, rubber, plastics, and beverages), trade (including tourism), and financial services (banks, insurance, and real estate). These three sectors alone contribute around two thirds of the city's income, and their domination has increased since the 1980s, especially trade and tourism. Other sectors of importance include social services, transportation, and construction. Many of Cape Town's most important industries draw on assets beyond the city itself. In terms of value, it is products from the wider region of the Western Cape Province, such as fruits, wine, and fish, that dominate Cape Town's exports.

▲ There are many vineyards in the area surrounding Cape Town, such as this estate at Montague. Once grapes are harvested, the wine is processed and aged in barrels (inset left) before being exported throughout the world.

Tourism

Tourism in Cape Town has increased dramatically since the end of apartheid, attracting around 800,000 international tourists and some 3.5 million domestic tourists by 2000. With its world-class hotels and stunning scenery, Cape Town frequently rates as one of the most desirable city vacations in the world. The majority of tourists visiting Cape Town are young (18 to 35), independent travelers, with less than a fifth coming as part of an organized package tour. The city government considers tourism central to the future growth and prosperity of Cape Town and is working with various groups to market local attractions.

Dual economy

In common with many less developed countries, Cape Town has a dual economy with formal and informal sectors. The formal economy is the official, regulated economy where people are formally employed and earnings, business transactions, and taxes are properly recorded. By contrast, the informal economy is characterized by small-scale and unregulated businesses that are not registered, deal in cash, and rarely pay any taxes. According to recent studies

64 percent of Cape Town's labor force were employed in the formal sector in 2002 while the informal sector accounted for around 18 percent (the balance were unemployed). The proportion of Cape Town's labor force working in the informal sector has grown by around 50 percent since 1991, when it represented just 12 percent of the labor force, and it continues to increase today.

Besides its importance to the city's labor force, the informal economy makes important contributions to the overall economy of Cape Town, accounting for an estimated 12 percent of economic activity. In reality the contribution may be considerably higher because the informal nature of the economy makes it very difficult to measure accurately. Some informal sector elements are highly visible—such as street hawkers selling goods or services in public places—but the informal economy also includes those who work in their homes or in small workshops and offices.

▲ An unemployed man making crafts out of wire and scrap metal to sell to tourists.

▼ A woman selling candy, chips, and apples—all typical of an informal sector street vendor.

▲ A woman learns how to make bread at CAFDA job creation project (see page 24).

Racial bias

Cape Town's informal economy is overwhelmingly dominated by the black population. It is thought to account for around 30 percent of all jobs held by blacks. This compares to a level of around 4 percent of white employment in the informal sector. The levels for the colored and Asian populations are estimated at 7 and 5 percent respectively. The high levels of informal employment within the black population are historically linked to the fewer job opportunities that were available to blacks during the apartheid era. The informal economy boomed in the townships in order to provide services for the large numbers of people forced to live in these overcrowded areas. Such services, together with trading, continue to dominate the informal economy, but agriculture, construction, manufacturing, and transportation are also significant. Future growth in informal sector employment is likely to remain dominated by the black population as internal migration of the unskilled black population to Cape Town continues—a pattern that began when restrictions on movement were lifted following the end of apartheid.

Changing fortunes

One of Cape Town's economic successes in recent years has been the Victoria & Alfred (V&A) Waterfront. This historic area was once the trading hub of the city and the main port area. By the mid-1980s the docks were falling into disrepair as shipping traffic was transferred to newer port facilities able to deal with the new supervessels used in today's global shipping industry. In 1988 a project was launched to revitalize the waterfront area into a mixed commercial, retail, housing, and entertainment district. Various groups in Cape Town (including representatives from industry, tourism, environment agencies, fisheries, and local government) were consulted before construction work began in 1989. Several phases

▲ New apartment buildings on the waterfront overlooking the working port.

of development (which is ongoing) have transformed the V&A Waterfront into a world-acclaimed model of city redevelopment.

▲ The Cape Town waterfront as viewed from the water with Table Mountain in the background.

Success story

The V&A Waterfront today boasts more than 1,800 hotel beds, 71 restaurants or eateries, 600 residential dwellings, and numerous shops, offices, museums, and entertainment venues. Some 20 million people visit the waterfront every year, a dramatic increase from the 5.8 million who visited in 1991. Around a quarter of visitors are foreign tourists, but the majority (around 60 percent) are local residents, proving that the development has been a real benefit to the city. It has also been an enormous benefit in employment terms, responsible for around 16,000 permanent jobs and almost 19,000 temporary jobs in 2003. More than 80 percent of these jobs are newly created rather than relocations, and 70 percent of them are low-skilled jobs, helping to relieve the city's unemployment problems. Furthermore, the V&A development has had a wider beneficial impact. For each new waterfront job, another two have been created within the Western Cape region to provide supplies and services to the waterfront businesses. Other inner-city areas have also been revitalized, with old industrial buildings becoming apartments, for example. This, in turn, is helping to attract people back into living in the city center and reducing the problems associated with urban sprawl, such as traffic congestion and pollution.

CASE STUDY

Integration for development

Sarah Moloto is the director of Cape Town's Integrated Development Plan (IDP). This is the plan that guides the municipal budget, and its goal is to create conditions that will alleviate poverty, promote local economic development, eradicate unemployment, and promote reconstruction and development. "People are vital to this process," Sarah explains, "and we have, for example, a mayoral listening campaign that gives communities across the city a voice in the planning process." Though there are many challenges in rebuilding a new integrated and post-apartheid city, the economy plays a central role. The latest version of the IDP emphasizes this fact, as Sarah points out. "Cape Town recognizes that in addition to growing the economic cake, it is as important that more of our people get to taste it."

Managing Cape Town

Cape Town covers a large area and has historically been managed by seven different municipal authorities, each covering a different part of the city and its surrounding area. In December 2000 the City of Cape Town Metropolitan Municipality was created to bring together these municipalities into a single governing body. This was part of a national project in South Africa to reform local governments and remove the barriers and divisions that were set up during the apartheid era. Citizens believed that a single authority for Cape Town would better be able to use resources across the entire city region. It should also help to reduce the inequalities between the different regions.

▼ The center of the city, including the docks, falls under the governance of the Cape Town Metropolitan Municipality.

▲ A public mural near the parliament buildings depicts the right of millions of South Africans to vote for the first time in the 1994 elections.

Unicity

The new united City of Cape Town, popularly referred to as the "Unicity," is governed by an elected 200-member council and executive mayor. The council consists of 100 elected ward councillors representing the city's 100 separate wards and 100 political party councillors who are elected by proportional representation. The full council is the highest decision-making power in Cape Town, but it hands certain responsibilities over to various committees and subcouncils.

Citizenship

At the core of Cape Town's new approach to managing the city is the participation and involvement of the people living there—its citizens. New structures have been established to make sure that all residents of Cape Town have access to "contact centers." These centers provide information about council programs or opportunities to talk to council officials about problems affecting local communities. In addition, city authorities have opened up planning to residents in the form of public meetings that are now held across the city. These invite residents to voice their concerns and contribute ideas toward the formation of the city budget or other important plans such as the city's Integrated Development Plan (see page 35). Thousands of city residents, many of whom have rarely had the chance to speak out before, have been attending the meetings and helping the Cape Town authorities to achieve their mission of "Building Our City Together." In a city with so many problems, the local government considers it essential to encourage and support local people to use their own skills and resources to solve problems facing their communities.

CASE STUDY

The Junior Council

Munowarah Rawoot is Mayor of the Cape Town Junior City Council (JCC) 2004–05 and heads its executive committee. This consists of 10 members, elected by the JCC. The JCC is itself made up of students from schools across Cape Town. The JCC, supported by the city government, provides a forum for young people to engage in civic and community affairs. Full JCC meetings, attended by an average of 350 young people, take place every two weeks. Munowarah explains that the JCC selects its own themes and program of meetings. "This year the theme is 'Junior City Council against Crime.' We want to take a stand against the high crime rate and consider what the solutions might be."

▲ More visible policing helps to reassure residents.

Tackling crime

One of the benefits that Cape Town hopes to gain by engaging more actively with its citizens is a reduction in crime. With such high levels of poverty and extreme inequalities, Cape Town has historically had serious crime problems. Crime is still a major issue today and remains much higher than in similar-sized cities in Europe or the United States. Greater efforts to provide opportunities for young unemployed people—those who often end up turning to crime in desperation—are considered essential to crime reduction. More visible policing is also a key policy, so that police become a regular feature of the community. A city police force has been established to support the national police by enforcing municipal laws, providing community safety, and regulating the city traffic. The presence of the city police has significantly reduced crime rates in city center and encouraged people to return there to live or to enjoy its facilities. It has also had a beneficial impact on tourism by improving the appeal and safety of the city for visitors. Additional policing is also being deployed in township areas to improve security in areas that have historically had no or very little policing. Community police forums and neighborhood watch programs are also in place to work with local people in making Cape Town a safer place to live.

◀ Police contact with local residents' groups has helped to improve relations and the quality of policing.

National government

Besides the local government, Cape Town is the seat of the legislative chamber of South Africa's national government. The legislative chamber is in charge of debating key national issues, of passing new laws, and of overseeing the executive chamber of the government. It is based in the parliament buildings at one end of the Botanical Gardens in the city center.

▲ The parliament buildings in Cape Town are the seat of South Africa's legislative chamber.

Sharing ideas

Cape Town is one of nine cities that make up the South African Cities Network (SACN). The SACN is a nonprofit organization that helps cities in South Africa to share experiences of good practice that are helping its cities become better places to live. In particular the SACN has helped to develop a model for its members based around a city development strategy that ensures cities are productive, inclusive, well governed, and sustainable. The SACN is a good example of how national cooperation can benefit cities facing similar difficulties. In 2005 the SACN began a process of expanding its activities to share ideas and lessons with other cities elsewhere in Africa.

▼ The proposed site of an urban renewal project.

You are now entering an

URBAN RENEWAL AREA

Together, building a stronger nation

CITY OF CAPE TOWN
ISIXEKO SASEKAPA
STAD KAAPSTAD

Transportation for Cape Town

Cape Town was established as a port for international shipping. The shipping industry remains important today, and Cape Town is on one of the world's busiest shipping routes between Europe and the Americas in the west and Asia in the east.

▲ The Cape Town docks area. The natural harbor has been an important center of shipping for centuries.

Port of Cape Town

Cape Town's modern port facilities are in Table Bay and consist of two main docks. In 2004 the Port of Cape Town handled more than 3,000 vessels with a total tonnage of goods of around 10.1 million tons. About 6 million tons of this was container traffic, and the remainder was bulk cargo such as grain or coal.

Cape Town plays a particularly important role as the main port for the export of South African fruit (apples, pears, oranges, grapes, and so on) and has developed special handling facilities for such fragile cargo. The port is also a major repair and maintenance center and services fishing, oil, and container vessels from all around the world. Passenger cruise liners also use the port's new docks. Smaller passenger vessels, however, continue to use the old docks of the Victoria and Alfred Basins.

▼ Cape Town's docks offer important ship repair services for both domestic and international fleets.

Globalization

With business and trade becoming ever faster and increasingly global, Cape Town International Airport is playing an important role in the future of the city. The majority of tourists arrive in Cape Town by air, and the airport, to the east of the city center, is also handling an increasing volume of freight. By 2004 the airport was handling more than 60,000 aircraft and more than 5 million passengers a year. By 2015 this is expected to increase to 14 million, and the airport will have to expand considerably to meet the demand. New terminal buildings will be connected to the main building by underground tunnels. The airport also plans to develop "Freight City" as a facility for handling and warehousing freight and an industrial zone to attract companies producing lightweight but valuable products, such as electronics and aerospace components.

National links

Vital to the success of Cape Town's port and airport are its connections with the rest of South Africa. These internal road and rail connections allow the flow of people and goods into and through the city.

Cape Town is on the main road artery to other key population centers, such as Johannesburg and Durban, and to rural areas. Cape Town also has well-established rail links connecting it to Pretoria and Durban and the key towns and cities in between.

Local transportation

Within Cape Town are various transportation options. Metrorail, the city's train system, provides a route for many commuters into the main business district of the city. The road network is also good but can become busy during peak travel periods. City buses serve many of the suburbs but are supplemented by shared minibus taxis that cover numerous routes across the city and work out to be a similar cost. Many people simply take whatever comes along first. Between them, buses, shared taxis, and the Metrorail account for 60 percent of all commuters in Cape Town. One unusual form of transportation in Cape Town is the "rikki." This is a small Asian-style van that can be booked or flagged down and offers transportation for several people to most places within the city center and immediate neighborhoods.

▼ A long-distance train leaving Cape Town.

▲ Trains are used to get to and from the townships, but they are considered unsafe after dark.

Disconnected

A legacy of Cape Town's past is that many of its poorest communities are today isolated from the city center, located in areas such as the Cape Flats that are up to 16 miles away. For the people living in these communities, travel can represent a significant cost and prove a barrier to job opportunities.

Walking is the main form of mobility in many of the townships, particularly where dwellings are too densely packed to allow vehicle access. Improving transportation so that marginalized communities are better incorporated into the city is a major part of Cape Town's future development plans.

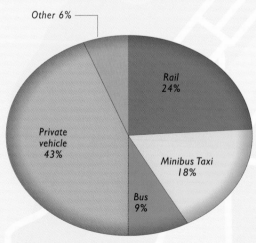

Other 6%

Rail 24%

Private vehicle 43%

Minibus Taxi 18%

Bus 9%

▲ Transportation in Cape Town by type (percent of total), 2003.

▲ The city center has a good network of street transportation.

◀ Shared minibus taxis gather in the city center. This is the favored form of transportation for most people, and many residents in the townships rely on them to get to and from work in the city center.

CASE STUDY

Klipfontein Corridor

Terence Smith is the project manager for the Klipfontein Corridor, an ambitious transportation plan designed to better integrate the Cape Flats region of Cape Town with the city center. Existing transportation options are congested, unreliable, and often unsafe. People can spend more than four hours a day and up to 60 percent of their income traveling to and from work.

The Klipfontein Corridor, which began construction in 2005, will connect Khayelitsha through Crossroads, Guguletu, Gatesville, Athlone, and Mowbray to the city center. Terence Smith explains the key features of the project. "A dedicated bus rapid transit (BRT) system, separated from private vehicles, will run buses every five minutes at peak times. Improved stations that are safe and protect people from weather will offer real-time information about when the next bus is coming. An integrated ticketing system will be used so that commuters can move from one mode of transportation to another without having to buy another ticket, and a whole network of safe pedestrian and bike lanes will feed into the BRT. The focus is on transforming the urban fabric and improving quality of life for people living along the Corridor." The Corridor is also expected to kick-start local development through the reconstruction of public spaces and the creation of day care centers, cafés, restaurants, commercial centers, and even cultural and sporting venues. The vision is that Klipfontein will become a destination rather than somewhere that people just pass through. Planners hope that roads and spaces that once divided and were the cause of much discontent will become roads to bring people together and spaces that unite.

Culture, leisure, and tourism

Cape Town has an extremely rich culture that not only represents its own varied population but also reveals its links with other parts of the world. Museums, theater, film, music, and art and crafts all feature prominently, and Cape Town also hosts numerous festivals and special events.

▲ Buskers entertain tourists on the North Quay at the Victoria & Alfred Waterfront.

Cultural center

Cape Town's museums vary from the District Six Museum, which considers the forceful eviction of people from this now-infamous community during the apartheid era (see page 15), to the Rugby Museum, which focuses on one of South Africa's most popular sports. There are also several historical buildings that today operate as museums, such as the prison on Robben Island, where Nelson Mandela was once held.

Theater is growing in popularity and there is normally a selection of comedies, short plays, and big blockbusters to choose from. Music is more popular than theater in Cape Town, and the city is well known for its jazz. In March each year, the North Sea Jazz Festival is held in the city and attracts some of the biggest names in the jazz world. Cape Town has also produced its own jazz stars, the most famous of whom is Abdullah Ibrahim (also known as Dollar Brand), who in the early 1960s recorded some of South Africa's first jazz albums with other South African greats like Hugh Masekela. Jazz is one form of music popular among all of Cape Town's racial groups, and it is as likely to be heard and played in the townships as it is along the trendy waterfront area. Rap, reggae, hip-hop, and local styles such as "kwaito" and "bubble gum" are among the other forms of popular music found in Cape Town, together with U.S., European, and other African acts.

Artistic talent

Cape Town is not short of artistic talent. The sculpture *Baobabs, Stormclouds, Animals and People* (below), which dominates the foyer of the Cape Town International Convention Centre, is among the city's best-known works. It was created by local sculptors Brett Murray and Tuoi Stefaans Samcuia of the !Xun and Khwe San Art and Cultural Project. It stands 24.5 feet tall and 92 feet wide and represents the diversity of South Africa. The townships are also known for their artwork, and Cape Town is particularly associated with beautiful beadwork that has its origins in the region's indigenous cultures.

CASE STUDY

Monkeybiz

Monkeybiz was founded in January 2000 by Barbara Jackson, Shirley Flintz, and Mataphelo Ngaka. The project supplies women in the townships with glass beads and cotton, and the women use them to make beaded dolls and other beaded crafts. Monkeybiz buys the finished products and markets them locally and internationally as artworks and souvenirs. The products have featured in exhibitions around the world and in top designer stores, such as The Conran Shop in London, New York, Paris, and Tokyo.

Monkeybiz has more than 350 women making dolls and a further 200 women who want to participate. Those involved have seen their incomes rise considerably and have been able to better care for their children, some of whom have gone back to school thanks to the income from Monkeybiz. The project founders also channel a large percentage of the profits into HIV/AIDS awareness programs. One of the most important benefits of the initiative, however, is the sense of pride that has been restored in many of the women who work with Monkeybiz. In the process, the project has helped to revive and expose the traditional beadwork of the Western Cape region.

A sporting city

Cape Town's location means it has sporting opportunities beyond those enjoyed by many cities. There are facilities for soccer, golf, tennis, swimming, rugby, and cricket. In addition, Cape Town has thriving water sports that include surfing, windsurfing, yachting, and diving. Climbing, mountain biking, rappelling, and skydiving are other outdoor activities that benefit from Cape Town's location. In terms of popularity, soccer is one of the top sports and draws large crowds that are only likely to grow as Cape Town prepares to be one of the host cities for the 2010 World Cup soccer finals. In Cape Town, the World Cup games

will be played at Newlands, Cape Town's international rugby stadium.

Although sports can be a unifying force, both facilities and participation (with the exception of soccer) remain overwhelmingly dominated by the white population. There are exceptions to this rule, however, and black Cape Town residents from the townships have represented South Africa in traditionally white-dominated sports like cricket and sailing. In 2007, for example, Marcello Burricks, a black Capetonian who grew up in the tough Slangkop township, will be part of South Africa's multiracial America's Cup

▲ Newlands Stadium is best known for hosting major rugby matches, but in 2010 it will become one of the venues for the World Cup soccer finals.

◀ South Africa's Andre Pretorius attempts a drop goal against New Zealand at Newlands Stadium in the 2005 Tri-Nations rugby series.

▲ Children enjoy an informal soccer game in Khayelitsha.

sailing team—the first time an African team will enter the prestigious competition.

New sporting facilities are also being established in township areas to create opportunities for greater integration through sports and leisure. The Swartklip Regional Sports Facility is one such facility. It will be accessible to residents living in Mitchell's Plain and Khayelitsha, two of Cape Town's largest and most poorly serviced townships. When completed, Swartklip Regional Sports Facility will support rugby, soccer, baseball, hockey, cricket, softball, basketball, and swimming.

Other proposals are smaller in scale, such as the initiative started by Ronnie Samuels, a Cape Town traffic officer. Annoyed with gangsterism in the Lavender Hill area where he lived, he set up the Olympic United Football Club (a soccer team) in 2004 to provide new opportunities for children living in Lavender Hill and reduce the risk of their becoming involved in the gang culture. More than 60 children are already involved in the club. They play matches against neighboring teams, and some players have been invited to an international event in Brazil.

▼ Unemployed youths hang around in Lavender Hill, a poor settlement where gang activity is reputed to be rife.

◄ The Two Oceans Aquarium is one of the many attractions on offer to tourists.

World destination

Cape Town today ranks as one of the top city destinations in the world and often beats New York, Paris, Sydney, and Rome in surveys on the desirability of world cities. A stunning natural environment, thriving and diverse culture, and relatively low cost provide a winning formula that Cape Town is eager to exploit.

The local government regards tourism as a core strategy in the future economic development of Cape Town, especially in the buildup to the 2010 World Cup soccer finals, which South Africa is hosting. Already new facilities are being put in place such as the expansion of the airport, newly proposed cruise facilities in the port, new hotels, and improved policing and security. All of these will help to draw more tourists to the city. Table Mountain and the V&A Waterfront receive the greatest number of visitors, but Cape Town offers many other attractions that it intends to make full use of. These include landmarks such as Robben Island, District Six, and the Castle of Good Hope; cultural attractions such as museums, theaters, and Cape Town's well-known music scene; and natural attractions such as the unique fynbos habitat (see page 50), a stunning coast line, and a rich sea life. Adventure tourism and ecotourism have been quick

◄ The cable car to the top of Table Mountain provides breathtaking views.

to take advantage of such natural assets and there are now walking, mountain biking, diving, water sports, and other specialist tourist activities on offer.

Tourism for the townships

Tourism is clearly of benefit to airlines, hotel owners, and tour operators, but it can have much wider benefits. Many people living in the townships have also been able to benefit from tourism in their city. In Khayelitsha, Langa, Masiphumelele, and other townships, township tours have been established to meet the curiosity of visitors interested in township life.

Restaurants, cafés, cultural centers, and gift shops have also sprung up to cater to these visitors. The demand for souvenirs is sustaining—and in some cases reviving—a range of traditional arts and crafts too. The townships, and especially their women residents, have been involved in producing goods for sale in the tourist markets, and in doing so they are helping to lift themselves out of poverty. Wola Nani (meaning "we embrace and develop each other" in Xhosa) is one such organization. It works with people infected with HIV/AIDS and produces quirky and attractive gifts including decorated light bulbs, papier-mâché bowls, and jewelry, much of it using recycled raw materials found locally.

CASE STUDY

Cape tourism

Bess Copeland is from England but is studying for a year in South Africa. She is today heading out to Robben Island where Nelson Mandela was once held as a political prisoner. "Nelson Mandela has always inspired me, and I saw him speak recently at a 'Make Poverty History' meeting in London," explains Bess. "I wanted to visit Robben Island to see this important symbol of the struggle against apartheid. It is important for tourists to understand this struggle when they visit Cape Town. It is easy to do typical tourist activities such as visiting the Cape vineyards and the waterfront, but I want to see the real Cape Town, to learn more about the issues facing the majority of people living here. Cape Town is a beautiful city and it is perhaps easy to ignore the incredible inequality and ongoing poverty when you are visiting, or even living here, as a white person. But tourists should make it their responsibility to experience something of the reality for most people living here."

The Cape Town environment

Cape Town is located in an area of rich, and in some cases unique, natural habitat. Its coastal waters are some of the most fertile in the world and support a wealth of marine wildlife—more than 10,000 species in total. These include several whale species, dolphins, Cape fur seals, African penguins, and the famous great white shark.

Moving inland, Cape Town also boasts the Cape floral kingdom, or fynbos, as it is also known. This is the smallest of the world's six floral kingdoms but also one of its richest, with some 7,700 plant species at a higher concentration than even the Amazon rain forest. The main species are Cape reeds, proteas (the king protea is South Africa's national flower), and ericas (heathers). There are some 600 ericas alone within the Cape floral kingdom, compared with just 26 in the rest of the world. A key feature of the fynbos is that so many of the plants (up to 70 percent) are endemic, meaning they are found nowhere else in the world.

▶ The king protea, South Africa's national flower.

▼ Fynbos habitat on the Cape of Good Hope.

Under pressure

As Cape Town's population has grown, so has the demand for land and other natural resources such as water and timber. A large population generates high levels of waste and pollution that can find their way back into the environment. The pressures are particularly acute in Cape Town because the city is surrounded by very rich, but also very fragile, habitats. Some species in the fynbos can be so localized that clearing an area of land big enough to build a house could make a species extinct. Several species of reptiles, birds, and mammals have become extinct in recent years due to pressures on their habitat.

In 1998 Cape Peninsula National Park (CPNP) was created as the centerpiece of Cape Town's biodiversity efforts to preserve species such as the African penguin. The new park brought fragmented areas of protected land together under a single managing authority and ensured that Cape Town's environment would be given the same level of protection as South Africa's other national parks.

▲ Penguins are a surprising sight for tourists expecting more "African" wildlife.

One CPNP program has been the introduction of a penguin crossing in Simon's Town near Boulders Beach. The beach forms part of the CPNP and has been very effective in protecting the African (or "jackass") penguins: In 1982 there were just two breeding pairs, but the colony today numbers around 3,600. Despite this, the penguins are still under under threat and need protection.

▲ Penguins at Boulder Beach are now protected as part of the Cape Peninsula National Park.

Speeding motorists are a key cause of penguin deaths: Cars often hit the penguins as they cross main roads to find inland nesting sites. It is hoped that the crossing, together with the introduction of artificial nests within the park, will reduce penguin fatalities.

Public education is playing a key role in protecting Cape Town's biodiversity. The destructive potential of visitors who roam beyond dedicated paths and of fire are being addressed in this way. Park and city authorities are also using more direct action, including a program to remove alien species that pose a threat to the fynbos.

Where is the water?

Water supply is a major environmental problem for Cape Town. The city is almost completely reliant on rainfall storage in 11 reservoirs that surround the city. In recent years increased demand for water (due to population increase), combined with below-average winter rainfall, has led to severe drought. The city has introduced water restrictions in order to conserve

dwindling supplies and embarked on a public education program with local communities and businesses to use water more efficiently. Communities have responded well and by February 2005 their actions had helped to reduce citywide demand by around 15 percent.

Public education is important, but in the longer term new solutions also need to be found. An additional rainwater storage facility—the Skuifraam Dam, being built on the Berg River—will increase supplies to Cape Town from 2007 and meet expected demands until around 2013. Beyond that the city authorities are investigating the possibility of extracting water from aquifers underneath the mountain chain that includes Table Mountain. Recycling of water will also play an important role, with wastewater being reused for irrigation and some industrial applications. This will initially come from municipal sources such as water treatment plants, but if successful it could be extended to commercial and residential gray water (water that has been used but is not dangerous).

▼ A reservoir outside the city showing low water levels.

▲ A clearly visible smog hangs across this Cape Town skyline. Air pollution is a major problem for the city.

Cleaner air

Cape Town's air is historically quite clean and healthy. The Cape Doctor, a wind that blows across Table Mountain toward the ocean, is so called because it sweeps the city's stale and polluted air out to sea. Air pollution is still an issue, however, particularly pollution with particulate matter—small particles created by using fossils fuels and fires. Particulates tend to reduce visibility and create what is locally known as a "brown haze" over the city.

This haze is most prominent in the winter months, especially in the Cape Flats region around Khayelitsha and the airport, where visibility can be so poor that pilots cannot see clearly and aircraft have to make instrument landings. Increased monitoring of air quality is helping city authorities identify the pattern of air pollution, and planners are currently preparing a strategy to reduce pollutants and clean up the city's air.

▼ On some days pollution can be so bad that Cape Town is barely visible from a distance.

Less waste

Cape Town currently generates around 6,600 tons of garbage every day—enough to bury four football fields under 3 feet of trash! More than half of this waste comes from industry and commerce (55 percent), with 30 percent from domestic sources and 15 percent from sewage sludge. Cape Town's waste is disposed of in six landfill sites. These are filling up rapidly and four of them are expected to be closed by 2008, leaving the city with a major waste-disposal problem.

A new landfill site is currently being researched, but the city's ultimate goal is to reduce the amount of waste going into landfills. A "Waste Wise" campaign has been implemented in schools, communities, and businesses to address the issues of waste reduction, reuse, and recycling. More than 100 schools, 5,000 students, and 800 teachers have been trained in waste education, and another 1,000 community stakeholders have been trained to take the Waste Wise message to almost 80,000 residents. City authorities have also started the Integrated Waste Exchange (IWEX) program. This identifies waste products from businesses and industry that could be used as a raw material by other businesses. Household recycling, materials-recovery facilities, and municipal composting have also been introduced.

Despite some success in all of these initiatives, however, the amount of waste going to Cape Town's landfills continues to increase, rising by 7 percent in 2002 alone. In addition, illegal dumping and littering are growing problems. Abandoned trash is not only visually unattractive and a health hazard but also uses valuable city funds when it is cleaned up. High-income households are a particular target for waste reduction. Their trash can contain 60–70 percent packaging waste. By contrast, the waste generated by Cape Town's low-income residents is about 80 percent organic and is therefore much easier to dispose of.

▲ A landfill site near False Bay. Cape Town is running out of space to dispose of its growing waste volume.

Community recycling

Across Cape Town, many people have decided to do something to improve the city environment. One such person is Michelle Sholto-Douglas, who used her own money to start a small community recycling project on a piece of land donated by the military. She has been able to afford to hire two workers who help with the sorting of the waste into different materials. The project reclaims metal, glass, paper, and other materials and also demonstrates home composting for organic waste. Michelle also uses the experience gained through her small project to provide environmental education in local schools. Reaching today's generation with such messages is a vital contribution to sustainable development and teaches individuals to take responsibility for their own actions.

▲ Michelle Sholto-Douglas demonstrates home composting for organic waste.

▼ Bottles are sorted at Michelle's recycling project. Michelle provides employment for two temporary employees who would otherwise be unemployed.

The Cape Town of tomorrow

Although apartheid officially ended more than a decade ago, the social, economic, and cultural divisions that were established over a 40-year period are a lot harder to dismantle. There is closer integration in some areas, such as at the University of Cape Town. Once the preserve of whites only, this is now open to all students, no matter what their ethnicity. In areas such as housing, recreation, employment, and education, however, Cape Town remains remarkably divided and there is still widespread racism.

Removing the barriers between communities to allow more integration is considered essential to the future of the city. City authorities hope that projects like the Klipfontein Corridor (see page 43) will act as a catalyst to real change and help to attain the goal of a truly united city. Unification will help reduce crime in the city by allowing more of its residents to share in the prosperity that the city has to offer. Greater security will in turn encourage more tourists and new investors into the local economy.

Sustainable development

Officials of the City of Cape Town are still getting used to working as a single metropolitan body but believe passionately in the future of the city and draw great strength from the many positive examples that are already in place. Through their Integrated Development Plan and their consultation with local communities, the city authorities have set out a vision for the City of Cape Town in 2020. This vision sees Cape Town as an inclusive city with citizens at the forefront, working with each other and with the city to achieve a common good. It also envisions Cape Town extending its influence nationally and globally as a city known for its leadership in Africa and the developing world. Sustainability is central to the city's vision, and planners are determined to conserve the region's unique ecosystems for future generations of Capetonians and visitors to enjoy.

To realize this vision the city has set a series of goals to be achieved by 2020. These goals are many (see box on facing page), and they set specific targets for each of a range of issues facing the city. Cape Town has devised five interrelated themes that will serve as the strategies through which the city hopes to realize its goals

▼ Students of all races relax between classes at UCT. Such multiracial scenes have yet to become common in Cape Town, however.

▲ Cape Town's International Convention Centre is helping to attract an international business community to the city and boosting Cape Town's global status.

and meet its vision. The themes are: to work toward a more integrated human settlement; to promote economic growth and job creation; to improve access and mobility; to build stronger communities; and to make services efficient and equitable across the city. These themes fall within a broader commitment to ensure that all future development is sustainable.

Cape Town has made much progress in its development since the end of apartheid, but rapid population growth and historical legacies have also hindered the speed and extent of this progress. To achieve the 2020 vision as a sustainable and global city, Cape Town must make the best use of its most valuable resource—its citizens, the people of Cape Town.

Cape Town's goals for 2020

- To improve key human development indicators such as literacy, poverty, and life expectancy at birth by 100 percent.
- To reduce the proportion of people living in informal settlements to less than 5 percent of the population. In 2003–04 it was around 10 percent.
- To provide everyone with access to basic services such as electricity, water, sanitation, and health clinics.
- To reduce the levels of violent crime by 90 percent.
- To reduce water use and the generation of waste by 30 percent.

- To provide everyone with access to a safe green space within walking distance.
- To promote and invest in renewable energy to become 10 percent of the total energy consumed.
- To double average real incomes and reduce levels of inequality between the rich and the poor.
- To reduce unemployment to less than 8 percent of the workforce. In 2003–05 it was around 20 percent.
- To improve literacy so that 95 percent of the population can read and write.

Glossary

AIDS Acquired immunodeficiency syndrome, a fatal immune disease resulting from HIV infection. Expensive drugs can keep people alive, but there is no cure.

apartheid A political system introduced to South Africa in 1948 that separated communities according to race and gave privileges to people of European origin. A new constitution in 1993 ended apartheid.

British Empire One of the largest empires in world history. By 1921 Britain controlled around a quarter of the world's land area, which was then home to around a quarter of the world's population.

Cape Flats The region east of central Cape Town, where large townships of poor black and colored residents are located.

colored The South African term for people of mixed race. This term is not in accepted usage in other Westernized countries.

formal economy The official, regulated economy, in which people are employed and earnings, business transactions, and taxes are properly recorded.

fynbos An ecosystem found in the Cape Town region with thousands of unique plant species; also known as the Cape floral kingdom.

gray water Used but uncontaminated water such as that from tubs and sinks or roof runoff.

HIV Human immunodeficiency virus, a virus spread by unprotected sex or contaminated needles or blood supplies that can develop into AIDS.

informal economy The unofficial economy dominated by small businesses or individuals that are not registered, deal in cash, and rarely pay any taxes.

informal settlement An unplanned settlement with few or no services (water, sewage, electricity) and often built using scrap materials.

infrastructure The basic structure of an organization or a place, for example communications and transportation.

legislative Relating to the writing and passing of the laws that govern a country.

municipal Relating to a town, city, or other region that has its own system of local government.

particulate matter Dust and particles released into the atmosphere from vehicle exhausts, factories, and other sources.

Pass Laws Restrictions introduced in 1952 that limited the movement of black and colored people living in South Africa.

pondokkies The local term for Cape Town's informal settlements.

proportional representation An electoral system in which political parties participate in the government in roughly the same proportion as their percentage of the total votes.

rikki A small Asian van used as a form of cheap local transportation in Cape Town.

rugby A form of football originated in Scotland in which no time-outs or player substitutions are allowed.

SACN (South African Cities Network) An organization in which several cities in South Africa share information about common problems and ideas about how to overcome them.

SARS (Severe Acute Respiratory Syndrome) A highly contagious disease that emerged in Asia in 2002 and spread quickly as people traveled around the world.

township A settlement formed during the apartheid era for people of black or colored racial origin to live.

Unicity A single authority introduced to Cape Town in 2000 to replace the several separate authorities that had governed different parts of the city until that time.

urbanization The process by which a country's population becomes concentrated into towns and cities.

Further information

Useful Web sites

Cities Environment Reports on the Internet
http://ceroi.net/cle/
An interactive site that allows visitors to decide how to live in the city then see the impact of their decisions on the city environment.

Statistics South Africa
http://www.statssa.gov.za/census01/html/default.asp
Up-to-date statistical information on South Africa, including data from the 2001 census.

Victoria & Alfred Waterfront
http://www.waterfront.co.za/
Progress and further plans for redeveloping Cape Town's historic waterfront.

Wola Nani
http://www.wolanani.co.za/skills.htm
Information about the organization's craft project, which generates income for women in Cape Town infected with HIV/AIDS.

Books

Domingo, Vernon. *South Africa*. Modern World Nations series. Philadelphia: Chelsea House, 2004.

An illustrated guide to the history, geography, government, economy, people, and culture of South Africa for readers grades 6 to 12.

Hamilton, Janice. *South Africa in Pictures*. Minneapolis: Lerner Publications, 2004.

A photographic tour of the history, culture, and society of traditional and modern South Africa.

Langley, Andrew. *Cape Town*. Great Cities of the World series. Milwaukee: World Almanac Library, 2005.

A photo-filled introduction to the history, landmarks, culture, people, and economy of the city.

Masekela, Hugh, and D. Michael Cheers. *Still Grazing: The Musical Journey of Hugh Masekela*. New York: Crown, 2004.

A biography of the legendary South African jazz musician; for older readers.

Index